DARK ABSENCE

Luis Enrique García

All rights reserved. The total or partial reproduction of this work is not allowed, nor its incorporation into a computer system, or its transmission in any form or by any means (electronic, mechanical, photocopying, recording, or otherwise) without the prior written permission of the copyright holder is a violation of these rights and may constitute a crime against intellectual property

The content of this work is the responsibility of the author and does not necessarily reflect the views of the publishing house. All texts and images were provided by the author, who is solely responsible for their rights.

Published by Ibukku, LLC
www.ibukku.com
Graphic Design: Diana Patricia González J.
Cover Design: Ángel Flores Guerra B.
Copyright © 2023 Luis Enrique García
ISBN Paperback: 978-1-68574-543-1
ISBN eBook: 978-1-68574-544-8

TABLE OF CONTENTS

EVASION	5
RESURFACE	8
IN YOU, AND IN YOUR FACE	11
HOURS GIRD	14
YOUR IMAGE	17
DAILY	20
WHEN	23
IN THE WAKING MORNING	26
I HAVE THE BLUE HEART	29
YOU IGNITE	31
PERSIST	33
IT'S YOU	35
YOU SHINE	37
I SENSE YOU	39
YOU	41
WHAT NOSTALGIA	44
YOU ARE WITH ME	46
I AM A RIVER	48
DARK ABSENCE	50
IN THIS HOUR	53
YOUR LIPS	55
ENEDINA	57
YOUR DEATH	60
IN THE BLEEDING ARMS	63
YOU ARE SEAGULL	66
I GREET YOU	68

EVASION

I am Edgar Allan Poe, I am the rebellious and modern arm,
Of the vibrant and red letters, from the United States,
I am a bleeding tree that distills eternity,
I am Golden Sword, Shield of Light,
Symbol and unstoppable trace,
And incendiary in America and the world.
I am Rubén Darío, the Giant Poet,
Seagulls of lightning crown my name,
And Stars of Gold, and Rainbows with Wings,
Emerge from the face of my voice, flag of light, and emerald codex,
That unclothes and embraces the heart, of the Planet.

I am a mighty and blue river,
That sings a new incendiary verse.

You can call me Edgar Allan,
Rubén Darío or Luis Enrique García, I am a river of blonde light
Lush and naked, and pregnant with eternal poetry.
I am an eternal dolphin, and wandering pilgrim,
That crosses the strident sea, of the centuries.

Every day I kill myself, in my incendiary voice
of black summers, and moist from your blue presence
and you resurge like an emerald plume,
in the abyssal pit of your light silence,
strident and lush,
and you furrow me with portentous peace,
and with uncontainable tenderness,
which is contagious of you, of your presence,
and of your sublime voice, which becomes fire,
and you sow your existence,
above mine, like the sea
covers with freshness and softness,
the smiling face of a port,
that snorts and sings lonely,
when the day peers and wrings,
its plume of colors,
above my being, and your life,
that it fertilized, and left existence,
that dreams daily, and widens
infinite, like an unstoppable sea,
and portentous, that dances and plays eternal…
From yourself, you evade, and you escape,
like a blue river, that is born unstoppable,
and sings with its naked voice, and runs
portentous, towards the sea that bursts,
and swings infinite in the distance.

Dark Absence

You are lightning life,
that flees from itself,
and claims eternal eternity,
above the hours and the centuries,
that pulse your intangible being,
that I have lost, and that dwells,
in the deepest part of me...

You are like a distant ship,
that approaches, and imposes itself eternal,
in the sea of my consciousness,
that trembles, and clings to your memory,
and to your sublime presence,
that I miss, and that loves me,
with your voice of silences,
and your naked, incendiary smile,
and eternal, that splendidly shines,
every time I burn,
in your eyes bare of innocence,
and you embrace me with a tenderness
incendiary, that I discover daily...

RESURFACE

Daily you resurface,
and you set me aflame with you,
with your sublime presence,
and ephemeral, that claimed eternity,
and shines victoriously, invincible
and subtle, like the breeze of the
sea, before the incendiary face,
of the days, where I love you,
I miss you, and I sense you,
with your skin of golden crystal,
and your portentous tenderness,
that spreads shared loves,
that widen, like a horizon
that smiles, furrowed by blue eagles,
and snakes with brittle wings,
in the shadowy eyes, of my naked love...

Dark Absence

In the warm and eternal nights,
that shine like the skin of your soul,
when I sleep surrendered and lonely,
and I flee unconsciously from myself,
and I recover you, surprised,
with the magical splendor,
of the palpable memory of your presence,
that I lost yesterday. And you ignite,
daily, above my dismembered voice.
I never lost you,
because you resurface and dwell
indestructible and eternal,
in the infinite eyes,
of my blue voice, that sows your image,
above forgetfulness, and your fierce absence,
which becomes eternal, where I dismember,
and break, distances and silences...

And I sense you here, by my side,
and you converse with me, loving and tender,
and I flee from the pestilent, hollow life,
on the light wings of smiling poetry,
which spreads, glorious, and uncontainable,
anointed with blonde stars
and blue springs, that infect with grandeur,
where I love you, and I see you, when I sink into you,
and I lose myself, in the mist of pale innocence,
and you resurface, from the deepest part of the forceful,
and dark river of my soul, because I am a fainting
and bleeding tree, that exudes slippery nostalgia,
that bleeds out the days, while I love you, and suffer, without you,
incendiary of your face, and of your name, which echoes,
and which spills light and darkness, at the same time,
that you ignite, in the divine eyes, of my dark love,
for your absence of centuries, that you vomit...

IN YOU, AND IN YOUR FACE

In you, and in your face,
I sink the soul, at every moment,
that I love you, and you become eternal.
You are a protective and faithful angel,
that guards my existence.
You caress my forehead, and my plume,
and you pour your heart, atop
my being, and the ephemeral skin,
of the silence that sails,
and girds, this naked ship,
that rests quiet and dreamy,
upon the blue waters,
of my own dream,
that widens and comes undone,
when I wake lonely,
and lean the past, upon the present...

You are a lightning that shines,
and becomes eternal, forever,
you are a river that sings silently,
with its voice pregnant with memories...
And in the quiet voice of the poet,
a spark of your magnificent being,
you burn eternal, and triumphant,
upon the face of nostalgia,
and on the eternal lips of love,
with which I love you, and lose myself in you.
And although sometimes, I cry,
because I am buried daily,
in the dark and bitter grave, carved by your absence,
you are a geyser of martyr light, that resurfaces
and sings unrestrained, from the soul,
and you hug me imperceptibly,
and silently, with your lightning voice...

Dark Absence

It's you, who stands before
between the past and the present,
and above, my voice belted with nostalgias,
and the fiery memory of your being,
that blossomed and fell withered,
in the midst of a fiery sea
of silences, that blows eternal,
and leaves surges of adventitious light,
incendiary and fraternal, on the lips of my love,
which undresses, and sings silently
and blue, to your lush memory,
that forges blonde empires, in the soul...

HOURS GIRD

Hours gird, my
loneliness, and your silence.
And your face, fiery with light,
here in the soul. The days
undress, and impose themselves ephemeral,
with their infinite body that smiles,
and dissolves in magical splendor.
And you expand, and become eternal daily,
on the bare and eternal shore,
of my soul, that sings to your presence
lost that I sense, at every moment,
that I sink into your name, and into your
voice, that resurfaces, and catches fire
eternities, in the bare eyes
of my soul, that embraces
the echo of your lost voice, that I recover,

Dark Absence

in your equidistant absence,
that intoxicates my voice
with dark winters
that eternalizes your absence, that shines triumphantly,
above the infamous and blind life,
that sowed hungry hurricanes,
upon your being, and your enormous beauty,
that shines, and embraces my infinite heart...
I sing to you,
with my voice of tenderness,
with this bleeding and pale voice,
of dark-loneliness, for having lost you,
from the day I lost you, when
you left, quiet and silent,
to the transparent region,
of eternal stillness, and silence...

Let me sing to you eternally,
with this uncontainable and broken voice,
of nostalgia. And in the blue echo,
of my wild and portentous soul,
which clings to not losing you,
despite that I have lost you.
And your words, your face painted
with light, and your presence, become eternal
and you shine, every time I
love you, and I sense you eternal,
very close by my side, and in the soul...

YOUR IMAGE

Your image is reflected,
on the bare face
of my soul. The silence,
spreads like a sea,
above my being, and your presence
fades, and resurfaces eternal,
in every moment, that I breathe
your name, and that I love you,
in this incendiary,
and wild solitude, that bleeds the days,
and the soul of my voice, opens its eyes
to the lost yesterday, and I see you,
and I sense you in my existence...
Loneliness ignites,
upon my skin, and your silence,
which dismembers and explodes daily,

like the cry of the sea, in the distance,
like a rose falling apart,
in the wild hands of the wind.
You emerge from the blue lips,
of the love in my soul, which trembles
and writhes inconsolably,
each time you ignite,
in the bare eyes of my soul…
And you resurge from everything, and from nothing,
from the soul of unstoppable remembrance.
It is you, who guides and illuminates
my destiny, at every moment
that I lose myself, and that I sink,
into my own defeat that I forge,
and sometimes rebuild,
when I see, without looking, the terrible
destruction I create daily,

Dark Absence

without unveiling the haughty body of silence,
that cowardly strangles the words,
and I destroy myself,
and my shameful and blind attitude betrays you,
each time I sink,
into a putrefied and lilac sea,
of pestilent shadows,
and you exist in the deepest part of me,
like a smiling and blue spring,
in the young skin of the soul, and your silence…

DAILY

Daily you ignite,
and eternalize, on the dark lips,
of the love that roars and sets ablaze
upon my chest, and in the soul.
Days smile and sing hymns
of nostalgia, with their dismembered
and dark voice. And you reflect, calm
and eternal, on the face of my words,
and your unerasable absence, strangles me,
and suffocates the hours, in which I exist
because I am dead, while I live...
And you paint my entire soul,
with blond rainbows, and blue lightning,
and you resurface from the depths of my voice,
and my conscience, that evokes your being of light,

Dark Absence

and your words make an
uncontainable roar, on the dark and broken skin,
of silence, that pulses and girds my days,
with your presence. And your heart becomes gigantic,
and undresses, and tears, kneels,
and spreads like ennobled,
and broken fog, among the 10 beloved trees,
of your orchard, because they are part of you,
and sprouted from your sacred
and fertile body, as a seasoned offering,
made by the portentous
and blue hands, of the omnipotent fate king,
who vomits eternity, and triumphs,
above the face of barbaric centuries…
And you intoxicate me with yourself,
with your blue tenderness,

and in the sublime voice of silence,
you shine daily, and re-emerge
eternal, with your loving voice,
unmistakable and subtle. And on the
broken lips, of the poem I write to you,
you bloom fiery and sublime.
You are like a bouquet of lightnings,
that explodes and makes a rumble,
uncontainable and fleeting,
upon my chest, and the fiery face
of ephemeral days,
that crown my temples, with your
absence that girds, and embraces my being,
with your eternal presence that I worship…

WHEN

When I submerge my name,
in a dark sea, of wild
silences, that quarter my voice,
that joins the voice of your greatness,
your sublime presence eternalizes,
and you reflect in the face of my love,
and my words. And in the perpetual shedding
of the days, that explode and paint
with beauty, and fiery youth,
my being, you exist in the soul
of the hours, while I exist
and die daily, because of your absence.
And I navigate without a compass, and without an exact destination,
through the rotten waters, of a blind,
and wild sea, born from my voice, slave
and prisoner, of my own apocryphal paradise,

and i dismember and spit infamously,
the harangue, of the great blue tiger,
hero and savior, of the blind world,
that exists without existing precisely,
and runs swiftly to the dark precipice,
that strangles and bleeds, its greatness.
And in the strident cry,
of my soul, that screams,
and that explodes in silence,
for having lost you,
that day I lost you,
when you left submissive,
and resigned, to the blue shore,
of eternal stillness,
and unbreakable hope,
where blue roses bloom,
that spill lightnings,
and blonde doves, and red jaguars, with wings

of tenderness, they hold your hand, your love,
and your words undress,
and you embody the divine will,
and the fruit perfected and exact,
despite the intrigue, and infamous vengeance,
of the unfaithful, destructive whirlwind,
that pierces the soul, and existence.
And your words, are lightning seagulls,
that fly and open their arms,
and you sow blue unicorns,
in the fertile land of your faithful promise,
and you pour out the sublime, and naked hymn,
that you wrote for me, the day of your departure...

IN THE WAKING MORNING

In the waking morning,
that gently stirs and silently smiles,
your face and your voice undress,
and eternally ignite in the soul.
And you invade me with your tenderness,
which blooms and eternally smiles,
and I sense you, in the swollen
notes, of my bleeding voice,
that bursts on the lips of silence,
which pours honor onto your
elevated presence, which I lost and recover,
every time I immerse myself in your face,
and in the eternal light, of your blue echo...

Dark Absence

And in the strident, eternal roar,
of my soul, that screams uncontrollable,
and vomits and sows, in the face of the hours,
rivers of bitter darkness, that strike
and savagely dismember, the tranquil peace
you gave me, remembering that I've lost you,
and that I love you, and it's impossible to resign myself,
to your fiery absence, and your subtle silence,
it eternalizes, girds me, and kisses my soul.
And in the warm voice, of your incendiary silence,
you furrow me with uncontainable tranquility, with promises of light,
and of love that sings, and spreads a blue tenderness,
that emerges and originates from your soul,
that shines and daily becomes immense,
every time your image catches fire,
in my eyes filled with gentle calm…

You, have offered the dreaming heart,
and painted it with rainbows with blue wings,
in sheer sacrifice and joy,
for the ten steeds, that were born
from your being, and that you forged selflessly,
peaceful and with commitment, by decree,
and will, of a sky that smiles,
and powerfully writhes,
every time it eternally gazes upon us,
ablaze with light, and with barbaric promises...

I HAVE THE BLUE HEART

I have the heart blue, and the voice dismembered,
and dark by your absence.
The day opens its infinite eyes, and on its wings
transparent of light, you splendor daily
and you become eternal. And in the eternal arms of love,
your image becomes an endless fire.
And you resurge by my side, and you paint me with tenderness,
and sublime dreams, the desolate
and dark existence, where I exist, and my soul bleeds,
for you, and for your wild absence,
that intoxicates my existence with eternal nostalgia,
that smells of solitude, without your incendiary presence,
that paints light ships, and universes of gold
in the soul, that roars and sows the heart,
on top of your name, and forgetfulness…

And in the warm voice of the days, which undress
and smile eternal at your subtle face, and your gaze of light,
precede and triumph daily, over forgetfulness,
and the dark nostalgia, that belts and beats the soul.
You infect me with yourself, with your incendiary love,
that sings and dreams, with lips pregnant with innocence,
and the naked voice, fiery, of dreams and shared promises.
And in the constant, eternal shedding,
of the days, which spill their colorful smile,
you ignite in my voice, and upon my
dismembered and dark chest, that sings solitarily,
and spills honor, to your lost presence,
which I idolize. And in a horizon pregnant with
stars, that smiles and undresses mightily,
on the naked lips of my soul,
your name, and your face become eternal…

YOU IGNITE

You ignite,
in my bare eyes,
and you traverse me with love,
with your sublime presence,
that awakens wild promises,
and lilac summers in the soul.
And in the breeze of incendiary peace,
that you leave me, your face, and your voice,
swing in my heart belted,
by floods of bitter shadows…
I am a blue seagull, running after you,
in the vivid memory, where you persist,
and you become a fire, atop my love,
and the present. And in the sway of the days,
that crown my soul with nostalgias,
my love and your love smile wildly,

and I sense your being of light, traversing distances in silence.
And you reflect in the soul, and in the quartered heart,
of the poet who smells of loneliness, and of eternal blue springs
that smile incendiary, and fragrant,
to your imposing body, which oozes eternity…
And in the fiery voice of your silence,
your emerald image, and the skin of your voice,
dazzle me, and you exist beside me, even though you are
far from me, having you in my eyes, and you absent.
And you dwell in the bitter and dark epidermis,
of the summer that dreams, with the hanged voice,
and the eyes pregnant with tenderness.
And I sense you, in the strident hymn, that ignites,
on the bare lips, of the rain, that rocks and wrings,
your plume of light, that smiles, before the presence of the rain,
that sings, and uncontrollably caresses everything,
and flees from itself, like you…

PERSIST

You persist daily,
and you become eternal,
in the dark voice of my soul.
And in the strident and bitter cry,
of my conscience, I embrace
your name. And your presence
slips through the walls
desolate of the fierce soul,
of the poet who spills incendiary
tenderness, eternities…
And in the harsh moments, that bleed
and dismember my soul, you persist in the fiery
echo, of my quartered voice,

that lights up with your subtle image,
and your words smile, and caress my heart,
and my face furrowed with darkness,
without you, because you have gone far,
and you dwell in the deepest part,
of my being, and my conscience,
that cries uncontrollably with nostalgia…
And you reflect, in the fiery and dark scream,
of my soul that bursts uncontrollably, with cold
nostalgia, that spreads, and strangles the soul.
And you bloom eternal, in the eyes of love,
and my silence, which you dismember, when I dialogue,
with your voice that distills silences, and your naked,
and fiery gaze, becomes eternal and smiles,
above my bitter voice that I reflect,
and eternalize, and that ignites,
in the middle of my love, and of your naked love…

IT'S YOU

It's you who accompanies me, and never leaves me,
in the fiery and cold solitude, where you persist,
loving and eternal, with a soul infected
with blue love, and your words caress my soul,
in a silence that barks and wrings my existence,
eternities, because you reemerge from the uncontrollable scream,
fiery, and broken, of my dismembered love,
that trembles and makes a clamor, like the anguished scream,
in the tender and wild voice of the rain,
thus you bloom and you set yourself aflame eternally,
in the infinite and blue eyes,
of a hungry and pale love,
for your fiery absence,
and with your echo of promises, you enlarge my life,
and you kiss my soul, eternities, every day that I exist...

And in my pregnant and broken voice, of ominous omens,
and triumphs that I long for, and desire to achieve with you,
for you, and for the blind life, that slips away,
over the victorious and eternal body,
of the centuries, you persist in me, and you spread
uncontrollable and subtle, like a strident lightning bolt,
in the withered voice of my soul,
and you impose, with your fiery presence…
And your blue silence, smiles, undresses and binds the soul,
with blue roses, and ships of gold.
You are sublime, and eternal poetry,
that roars and shines daily, in the naked voice of the poet.
You are a torch, you are a portentous plow of light
that illuminates, and opens furrows, in my existence.
You are a bouquet of lightnings,
you are a river of infinite kisses, that caresses,
and falls upon the skin of my soul, and of my lush love…

YOU SHINE

You shine in the fiery and broken smile,
of summer, which sings naked and fragrant,
its song of nostalgia.
And I sense you daily, and you ignite
in the dismembered eyes, of my blue soul.
You are a torch, lighting my existence,
at every step, and the omnipresent sun, that sheds
its colorful hairs, upon my being,
and my consciousness, that shouts and flows powerfully, after you...
I am a blue ship, filled with dreams, and promises,
that fights uncontrollably and triumphantly, against the dark shipwreck,
of the days, that I sail, and that batter my soul,
because you shine eternally, on my skin
fiery with solitude, and in the withered,
and naked voice of the poet, who sows the heart,
on the bitter shore, of my fertile and blue love,

and in your unmistakable presence,
that takes on eternity, and caresses me,
in the constant shedding, of my broken days, of darkness,
and disconnection. And you reflect eternally, and emerge powerfully
and subtly, from the deepest, of my dismembered and shadowy voice,
every time I sink, into you, and into your name that blossoms,
on the naked and blue lips, of my bleeding love,
with which I love you, and have your presence, which I idolize,
even though you have gone, and eagerly await,
the unknown day, of reunion,
that will uncontrollably meld, your existence,
and my existence, into one. You are a steed,
that distills flashes of gold, you cross,
and plow daily, the infinite shore of my soul,
that smiles and bleeds, for your dark absence,
that you eternalize, like a cloak of shadows and light
equidistant, in the emerald arms,
of my love hanged by black hurricanes...

I SENSE YOU

I sense you, in the piercing echo, of your own silence,
that barks and eternalizes your voice, in the clear crystal,
and naked memory, that cinches and triumphantly unifies,
your being and my desolate being, from that dark, broken,
and soulless day, when I lost you, when you triumphed uncontrollably,
above the sick, sanguinary, portentous,
blind, and pestilent deluge, that dismembered and devoured,
your existence,
day after day, and moved your presence away from mine,
in an instant...
And you dwell daily and spread, like eternal lightning,
oh butterfly of light, that peacefully and eternally plows,
the naked and blue comet, that engenders my soul,
that sings, writhes, and commits suicide,
and smiles while crying, distant from you,
and very close to your side, because I love you,
and you slide into my voice, you burn in the eyes of my blue love,
and spill a fire of bittersweet shadows...

upon my chest that adores you...
And you ignite, in my naked voice,
and in my eyes withered, by your absence,
that unites and fortifies, my presence with yours.
You are like the sun that smiles eternal, and tenderly kisses,
my face, and my being struck, by your absence that I obliterate,
and undo, every time I love you, and you slip away peaceful,
and eternal, in the arid eyes, of my soul,
and in the dark echo, of the verses that I write to you,
when I am alone, and I sense you,
and lean my soul towards the past, that saves,
tightens, and reunifies, my being and your being,
from the infamous
and fleeting forgetfulness, which I despise. And you reflect eternally,
in my heart, because you are an uncontrollable,
and barbaric fire, that becomes eternal,
in the naked face, of the blue words,
that the soul distills...

YOU

You never left me, despite your uncontainable absence,
for you dwell, in the pale region, of eternity,
and of precise life, and on the generous lips,
of a love that dreams, by your side, eternities.
The day opens its crystal eyes, and bares its body,
pregnant with scorpion lightning, and smiles with innocence.
And you reflect mightily, on the damp face,
of my words, which bloom and shine, for you,
each time I plunge into your visage,
and in the unmistakable echo of your voice,
that sets aflame my existence with memories...
The days sing, with a bleeding face,
and a voice, pierced and blind, of bitter deluges that strangle,
my heart, and the soul that evokes,
your presence that imposes itself daily.
And you gleam in my chest, atop forgetfulness and the cruel years,
that strip love bare, and hope kneels at my feet, and vomits
blond stars, into my hands, because you and only you,

are a waterfall of silences, that resurges,
and you gird my nostalgia with lightning, each time your
face, and your light-filled smile, slip
onto the dark wall of my soul...
And you re-emerge, incendiary and eternal,
in the naked and blue mirror,
of my soul, and in the dark voice of the tree, that extols,
and pours forth uncontainable and righteous honor, with the
sublime offering,
of the naked and broken verses, it writes to you.
You are light seagull, you are a river of blue stars,
that navigates uncontainably,
the infinite and childish prairie of my soul,
that sings in silence, to your precise presence that I regain,
each time you delve, into the soul,
and into the eyes of the ear of grain,
that kisses and tightens, your heart, in an eternal embrace.
You are an offered and beautiful rose, that smiles and sings,
upon beholding me, and you bloom daily and you expand,
like a sea of bittersweet lightnings,
you are a sky pregnant with blue unicorns, above my voice,
and your silence, incendiary, and bare, pulsates and echoes,

Dark Absence

in the deepest part of the dark mountain, of my chest,
and of the pestilent and sanguinary winter, that corrodes
and strangles, the haughty and proud face of the lightning earth,
that adores divine Jesus, and the chalice of blue gold,
that forges and shakes, planets and galaxies,
to the omnipotent and unique roar, of his lush and naked voice,
that forged your being, like a smiling palm tree, that dreams,
and opens its arms, to the destiny buried, in the wild claws
of the life of bitter dust, that I live, and that you lived,
on the eve of the flight towards the region
of infinite blue forests, that smile peacefully,
and the crystalline tenderness, slips from your incendiary,
and bare eyes, where my image
extends like an emerald sky,
that hangs and is born from your name,
crowned with springs, and lilac stars…

WHAT NOSTALGIA

What a deep and so dark nostalgia,
and these arms moist with loneliness,
for your so long absence that you eternalize,
and on the skin beaten by silences,
that pulse and anoint with smiling memories,
you burn daily, in the eternal face,
of my life, and in the bitter and broken voice,
that flows from the wide and raging river,
of my blue conscience, that evokes your being,
and your sensed presence, that infects with
eternity, and soft tenderness…
The hours and the days, ignited with promises,
for you, and to you, for your impalpable presence,
that burns, and girds with dark nostalgia,
the quartered heart of the blue steed,
that harvests and spills rose lightnings,

Dark Absence

on the lips, and in the deepest soul, above your name,
and in the bare, and deserted album, where I sow the soul,
in the dark verses I write to you, because you are distant,
and with me daily. Your absence bleeds me, and darkens,
the blue face of my voice each day is an endless century,
while I love you, and evoke you,
and uncontrollably wait for your return,
toward the destiny, that unites and separates, your presence
and my bleeding presence, from yours, in favor
of a paradoxical project, that magnifies the dream,
and the sublime love, that you inspire me, eternal,
with the tenderness that swells, and enlargens the soul,
and infects with you, with your silence pregnant with twilights,
you hold me tight, and you furrow my skin,
and the eyes hungry to look at you, although I enjoy
your unexpected presence, with a rain of
emerald stars, and blue plumes, which I sense,
and drain from your immaculate forehead,
which smiles triumphant and portentous…

YOU ARE WITH ME

You are with me from afar, incendiary of eternity,
in the pale and fresh, moist and subtle,
deserted and bare morning, of June that smiles in agony.
The clouds pour down kisses with tenderness, falling shattered,
upon my skin, and the infinite body, semi-desert and empty,
of this town I love, amid its invincible warrior arms,
that forge its indestructible greatness,
that daily grows and dreams. And you reflect in the soul
elusive, and in the smoky and eternal face, of the dark,
and pale voice of the poet, who begets and eternalizes horizons
with blue wings, in the bare codex, where I write,
and pour out the soul, in your honor that sings, and makes a racket,
upon the years and forgetfulness. The morning vomits peacefully,
its smiling and naked poetry,
mantle of light and equidistant shadow,
and pours daily, its infinite eyes, upon the world,
that melts and reunifies mightily, my presence with yours…

Dark Absence

And in the deep clamor, that barks unrestrained,
and sublimely reflects your victory, you drag me, ignite me
and infect me, with your exalted and martyr love,
and you furrow me with blue,
the voice of my conscience. Your eyes of light,
and your heart of fog, sings and writhes peacefully,
and solitary, upon my being and my name,
and my blue voice, which you mightily save,
from silence. And in the wet hairs of the rain,
and the subtle breeze, that intoxicates,
and dresses the landscape with freshness,
you burn eternal, in my voice,
and in the naked face of my soul,
that bares the withered heart,
upon the past and the dark present,
and I sow waterfalls of gold, and blue doves,
upon my arms. And my chest bares,
the masked day of the reunion…

I AM A RIVER

No, I am not alone,
because you dwell,
in the sea of my conscience,
and you resurge like emerald lightning,
in the echo of my withered voice.
You are a flag of light, and a book of fecund promises,
oh guardian tree
and protector who revives my senses, every time I falter,
and when I sink,
into my own darkness so deep that I spill,
into the days I live, without existing,
and your silence grows and smiles,
and merges your presence with mine, and you dismember
deluges of shadows that strangle, and strike the soul,
because I exist, and I am dead, without you…

Dark Absence

You are an uncontainable bouquet, of dreams that burst
eternal in the soul, of this dark stone, of solitude,
that traverses the wide tunnel, putrid, and terrible, of life,
that strangles itself, and destroys itself daily.
And with your hand of mist, and your face of incandescent light,
and your eyes, and your rainbow skin,
you save me from my own silence,
that sprouts masked and broken, from the soul, like a dark flower.
I am a river of emerald verses, I am a fecund promise
that shines, and that surged from the depths, of your womb;
and I flee uncontainable and portentous,
in the wide furrow of life,
that emerges from the lips of an incomparable and eternal god,
who pours life and death at the same time,
and who forged, this being that has never been yours,
and that was born of you, like a mantle of kisses,
incendiary, in the soul…

DARK ABSENCE

Your perfumed silence, smiles and encircles my voice,
with your presence, and you rain upon me like a breeze of light,
in the eternal arms of my soul that undresses,
and lives your silence of roses that endures and sings,
in my listless and bitter existence.
I am a ship of bittersweet shadows,
anchored by your name and your presence,
which I breathe and into which I sink in this dark,
putrefying empire,
where I live and die, slowly,
because you distill, your wild silence,
and I rediscover and sense your presence.
And in the moist, infinite, and gloomy veil,
that covers the face of a crystal star,
that smiles into the infinite, and up there,
the plume of light illuminates the world…

Dark Absence

Beneath the gaze of the spherical window that roars with splendor,
in the face of the strident thunder's bellow of rain,
that glides, and agilely releases its cold braid,
transparent and smiling, melting away,
before the violent and bittersweet bellow,
of your sublime, and fading self,
from whence this dreaming tree emerged,
quiet, from the depth of your womb,
and your beautiful, upright, and fertile geography...

Your elusive and dark absence, strangles
the ephemeral and fragile soul of days,
where I love you, and your bittersweet silence,
and incendiary memory of your eternal journey pierce my life.
You are like my own solitude, which accompanies me,
and eternalizes, atop my being, and your silence...

You are an infinite house, potent and majestic,
semi-deserted and dreaming, which smiles,
and eternalizes, its naked and blue smile;
your skin is furrowed with eternal rainbows,
and eyes pregnant with lightnings, which re-emerge
uncontainable, from the depth of your voice of silences.
I am a flash, of your being, that fell defeated,
and victorious, at the same time, you took on
eternity, atop your own death,
that liberates you from the ordeal, which you lived resignedly,
and with arms open towards an incomparable,
redeeming Christ, who rescues,
and exalts your existence...

IN THIS HOUR

In this hour of restlessness, and disconnect, your image
becomes eternal, on the naked, and broken wall of my soul
that daily darkens, remembering your absence that destroys,
the incendiary peace, that you leave, when you lived being dead,
in the midst of my arms, and of the blood set afire with loneliness,
and eternal nostalgia, which kneels, and spills
the heart, to your memory, before the almighty artist steed.
You are a dreaming rose, that lives set afire by silences;
allow me to sing to your lost presence, with the fragrant
and eternal aroma, of the verses I write to you unrestrained,
with the wounded and broken voice, of my soul, that closes its eyes
to the present, and opens the doors to the past.
I speak to you, oh unmistakable
and beautiful stela, with this voice that bows to the past,
because you reflect, on the face
of my voice, that wilts daily…

It's you, who caresses my soul,
and who destroys my pestilent nostalgia,
in the incendiary, and agonizing heart,
of the day, I sense you and you ignite,
eternal, in the youthful skin, and in the hair
warm and soft, moist with promise
and tenderness, of the wind, that rocks and squeezes
its infinite crystal plume.
And this being, a flash of your life,
And of your womb, daily,
crumbles and falls apart, for your absence
of centuries, that strangles and darkens
and suffocates my existence, and your name swings,
above my chest, and my soul,
both prisoner and free from the silence, that you distill…

YOUR LIPS

Your lips, painted with silences, intoxicate me
with blond summers, all the soul, and your being that
abandons me, finds eternity,
on the day of your unstoppable departure.
Let love widen, and dream
with naked eyes, and the soul open towards tomorrow,
and let it vomit blue surges, and hurricanes of light,
upon my dark weeping.
My incendiary presence, after the absence,
of your being, which daily becomes eternal,
and accompanies me, in the dark river of my existence,
that barks constantly at your departure, and at your silence
that strangles, my existence, and buries red stars,
in the soul, which writes the future,
with eyes pregnant with lightning…

You are a bittersweet light storm, that kisses me,
and the hanging sky, that resurges, and escapes
from itself; you caress my being, pulse my senses,
and bury my crying, in the naked heart of your love.
And your infinite presence rescues me from the terrible shipwreck,
where I plunge into the abyss, of my own
dark hell, where you save my life from death,
that I sense, every time I submerge
the heart, upon your name,
and your eternal and dark absence,
that bares the soul, of the faithful tiger,
that clings to your memory,
and I cannot fade you, from the sea of my consciousness,
because you ignite in my eyes, and in my voice,
pregnant, with barbaric silences…

ENEDINA

Enedina, you are the strident voice,
incendiary, and blue of the storm,
that resurfaces, and flees from itself;
and in the eternal echo of your candid voice,
I sense your presence, and the shadow,
of your disembodied being, that found
uncontainable and infinite eternity,
when you fled from your own body,
and you reach the Edenic and Blue Meadow,
where you smile with transparent skin,
and your naked eyes distill golden unicorns,
in your voice impregnated with eternal innocence…

In the ephemeral and bleeding body,
of the years, and in the pale, broken skin
of the days, you ignite and become eternal,
like a ship ablaze with dreams,
anchored in the eternal and blue arms,
of my soul, which evokes your being and does not forget you,
oh swallow of light, that re-emerges
like an unstoppable and eternal lightning,
from the depths of the voice of my conscience,
that barks, smiling at your memory,
that sets afire with dark nostalgia,
this withered and desolate flag,
that dies from constant agony,
due to your incendiary absence, which you eternalize…

Dark Absence

In your face of light,
and in your voice of rain,
fertile promises ignite,
that echo, scream, and clasp,
the naked heart of the days,
that kiss and caress eternally,
that strike and dismember,
this jaguar aflame with nostalgia,
that daily darkens, and bleeds out
uncontrollably, the face of my soul,
because your name, and your beautiful image,
blaze in my eyes,
and I feel you so close and so distant,
at the same time, that I cannot tear,
your voice, from my voice, that roars and explodes,
ablaze with memories, that pierce my existence...

YOUR DEATH

It is your fiery death,
and fugitive, like the summer
smiling, warm, and ephemeral
that sets my soul ablaze with tenderness,
because your name and your face,
become an unending fire,
on the blue, and broken lips,
and in the naked eyes,
of my unrestrained and shadowy voice,
like an eternal and wild surge,
of black lightning,
like a waterfall of seagulls
that crash, and fall,
shattered, upon my chest...

Dark Absence

It is your unrestrainable and portentous life,
that spills life, atop my life that's dead;
and in the broken skin, and in the bleeding face,
and damp with eternal nostalgia, and blue, of the days,
you ignite, in the dark echo of my voice,
that sings and embraces your name,
that caresses and wrings, my conscience,
beaten, by the dark winter of your absence,
that daily eternalizes, while I am
a poem written, with the dark tears,
of my soul that suffers, the farewell of your departure…

I am a desolate volcano,
with a dead soul,
I have skin set ablaze by loneliness,
and eyes sunk in your absence,
that strangles the incendiary body,
and smoking from the hours, that girdle
and pulsate eternal atop my being,
and from the eternal and blue silence,
that I spill in the clear present,
atop the unforgettable past,
that devours my life, before
the palpable body of reality,
that strikes down and devours the naked,
and eternal light that was on my face,
when today was a beautiful yesterday,
and your infinite absence, did not exist…

IN THE BLEEDING ARMS

In the bleeding and broken arms
of my lush, and pale voice,
your name grows gigantic and gleams,
like a spike offered,
to the portentous and precise life,
like a robust and hanging tree,
of my voice that sheds verses of dark light,
and naked letters that smile,
and caress daily,
my desolate being, and withered from loneliness,
that sows the heart, in your words,
atop the incendiary voice, of the silence...

Luis Enrique García

And you encircle with blue love,
that smiles uncontrollably and eternally,
you are the hope that smiles and dreams,
having you by my side, and these arms
girded by your absence catch fire
with wild tenderness, that I reflect and eternalize,
and your face of light, and the echo of your limpid voice,
that undress, the heart, and the wild promises
that I pour out for you, like a river
of thundering lightning,
and it flows over your sublime being,
and your voice laden with words of light…

Dark Absence

The day unveils its body,
which smiles, with tight skin,
and fiery with promises;
and you reflect in the soul,
and in the withered voice,
that I spill over,
your absence and your silence,
that sings and sows daily,
spikes of light, and blue eagles,
in my somber soul, which writes
and paints your unforgettable face,
on the bare walls of a love,
that my voice spills, remembering you,
and I sow the eyes, with wings
fiery with shared dreams…

YOU ARE SEAGULL

You are a blue seagull, that flies,
smiling, and free from the dark hurricane,
that struck, and constantly destroyed,
your immaculate being, when you existed
with me, and I could embrace you, so many times;
and I am part of you, and of your exalted being,
because I was born from the depths of your womb,
that left life upon the ephemeral life,
that runs impassioned and blind, towards the
abyss. I have a heart drunk with loneliness,
and you resurge, eternal and sublime like the sun,
above my love, and my infamous nostalgia.
You are reborn from the depths of my being,
and in the naked voice of the tower,
ignited with elusive loneliness…

Dark Absence

You have smiling stars, in your eyes,
and on the face, of my love, that sings to your memory,
I pour roses with my dark voice,
and tight with uncontrollable hope,
that cinches the heart, and the skin, of your lost presence,
that shines victorious, and that imposes itself eternal...
You resurge imposing everywhere,
above my love, and the dark landscape,
and wounded by nostalgia, without you,
due to your absence that bleeds,
my existence, my hungry words,
caress your face, and your heart,
ignited with uncontrollable eternity,
sings surrendered, and daily you shed,
eternally fiery memories,
that shout and burst portentous,
in a sea of bittersweet silences...

I GREET YOU

I greet you, with a soul aflame with agony,
due to your infinite absence, which chokes my days,
and compels me to fight, for myself, and for a world
of sublime grandeur, that I sense, and see,
and feel deep within me.
The day gently undresses, and in its pale,
and withered skin, and in the freshness of the clouds,
you blaze in my eyes,
and in my voice tight with shipwrecks.
And in the soft and tender hands,
of loneliness, you are reborn from yourself, oh martyr lark,
you impose yourself as an untouchable sky,
smiling, and bare, that watches me
with tenderness, and with love that distills,
and sows, blonde dolphins in my voice...

Dark Absence

The hours slip away, and dance like lightning,
over the pale landscape, of the infinite city,
of Guadalajara, where I rest, my temples, and my body belted
with sorrows, in the warm arms, ablaze with love,
of the goddess, and indestructible queen of Jalisco, who sings,
and vomits her soul, while I love you and sense you,
very close to me. And you silently and quietly observe the sublime
and beautiful city, legacy, and work of Charles V,
and you immerse your eyes
of uncontainable light, in this tree agonizing and dark,
for your infinite and bitter absence, that sinks me into a sea
that strikes, hurts, and bleeds the soul of the poet,
with infinite wild nostalgias. I am a lightning that emerges
boisterously, from your incomparable fertile womb;
I am a portentous plow and emerald, that opens a furrow,
in the fertile meadow of life; I am a solitary and blue ship,
that sails and contemplates, and challenges hurricanes…

www.ingramcontent.com/pod-product-compliance
Lightning Source LLC
LaVergne TN
LVHW041543060526
838200LV00037B/1110